# RED & WHITE QUILTS II

## 14 QUILTS WITH EVERLASTING APPEAL

Martingale®
Create with Confidence

Red & White Quilts II: 14 Quilts with Everlasting Appeal
© 2022 by Martingale & Company®

Martingale®
18939 120th Ave. NE, Ste. 101
Bothell, WA 98011-9511 USA
ShopMartingale.com

Printed in Hong Kong
27 26 25 24 23 22          8 7 6 5 4 3 2 1

Library of Congress Cataloging-in-Publication Data is available upon request.

ISBN: 978-1-68356-183-5

## MISSION STATEMENT

We empower makers who use fabric and yarn to make life more enjoyable.

## CREDITS

**PUBLISHER AND
CHIEF VISIONARY OFFICER**
Jennifer Erbe Keltner

**CONTENT DIRECTOR**
Karen Costello Soltys

**DESIGN MANAGER**
Adrienne Smitke

**TECHNICAL EDITOR**
Nancy Mahoney

**PRODUCTION MANAGER**
Regina Girard

**COPY EDITOR**
Melissa Bryan

**BOOK DESIGNER**
Angie Haupert Hoogensen

**ILLUSTRATOR**
Sandy Loi

**PHOTOGRAPHERS**
Adam Albright
Brent Kane

**SPECIAL THANKS**
*Photography for this book was taken at:*

• *The home of Jodi Allen, Woodinville, Washington*
• *Lori Clark's The Farmhouse Cottage, Snohomish, Washington*
• *The home of Tracie Fish, Kenmore, Washington*
• *The Garden Barn, Indianola, Iowa*
• *Happy Hollow Farm, Silvana, Washington*
• *The home of Julie Smiley, Des Moines, Iowa*

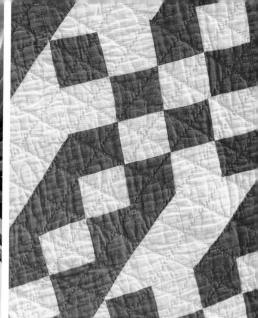

# CONTENTS

# INTRODUCTION

◆ ◆ ◆ ◆ ◆

What colors come to mind when you think of a classic combination? Do you have a go-to pair that you turn to time and again in your home, your wardrobe, or in your fabric stash? When we survey quilters (and especially fabric and pattern designers) about their favorite color combinations, red and white rises to the top of the list for many. For some it is the sharp contrast in hues that makes it ideal. For others, it's the freshness and playful way the colors pop against one another. And still others find comfort in the longevity of the pairing, with antique quilts aplenty that showcase the duo. For all those reasons and more, we all agree that the red-and-white color combination has lasting, timeless appeal.

Quiltmakers also often say that leaving a legacy and sharing their handmade creations with family are key reasons they enjoy their hobby. So we've married the two—classic quilts with lasting legacies—in a pattern book filled with ideas and inspiration for your home, your loved ones, and special occasions. Whether you're drawn to vintage looks or prefer a more contemporary feel, there's something inside for you.

How much of a purist you wish to be with your interpretation of red and white is up to you. Some patterns showcase the use of solids and invite plenty of opportunity for artful machine quilting in the open spaces. Others use tints and shades from ruby red to cherry red and bright whites to creamy neutrals. Some patterns are a scrappy mix of prints and stripes. There are quilts with borders and quilts without. What's your style: appliqué, medallion, or patchwork? It's here. The rule is, there are no hard and fast rules. You set your own. And by making these patterns your own, you'll be creating classic quilts to be enjoyed for the next century and beyond. Let's get started!

*~Jennifer Erbe Keltner*

# UNCHAINED MELODY

## SUSAN ACHE

*A master at turning the obvious into a "wait, what?" moment, designer Susan Ache is at it again. A symphony of stars surrounded by a diagonally set classic Irish Chain is what we see. But, in fact, it's 64 straight-set blocks set side by side with skinny sashing between the blocks and rows. Don't believe it? Read on to discover how she makes the impossible possible!*

**FINISHED QUILT: 83½" × 83½"**
**FINISHED BLOCK: 8" × 8"**

## Materials

*Yardage is based on 42"-wide fabric. Fat eighths measure 9" × 21".*

⅓ yard *each* of 16 assorted red prints for blocks

3⅓ yards of white solid for blocks, sashing, and inner border

2⅛ yards of red gingham for blocks

16 fat eighths of assorted light prints for blocks

¾ yard of red solid for sashing and inner border

2½ yards of red floral for sashing, outer border, and binding

7¾ yards of fabric for backing

92" × 92" piece of batting

## Cutting

*Cut the white strips carefully; you will not have any leftover fabric. All measurements include ¼" seam allowances.*

**From *each* of the assorted red prints, cut:**
1 strip, 2½" × 42"; crosscut into 4 squares, 2½" × 2½" (64 total)
4 strips, 1½" × 42"; crosscut into:
      6 strips, 1½" × 12½" (96 total)
      32 squares, 1½" × 1½" (512 total)

**From the white solid, cut:**
2 strips, 12½" × 42"; crosscut into 32 strips, 2½" × 12½"
22 strips, 2½" × 42"; crosscut *10 of the strips* into 256 pieces, 1½" × 2½"
18 strips, 1½" × 42"; crosscut into:
      32 strips, 1½" × 8½"
      260 squares, 1½" × 1½"

**From the red gingham, cut:**
5 strips, 12½" × 42"; crosscut into:
      32 strips, 2½" × 12½"
      64 strips, 1½" × 12½"
4 strips, 1½" × 42"; crosscut into 81 squares, 1½" × 1½"

**From *each* of the assorted light prints, cut:**
2 strips, 2½" × 12½" (32 total)
2 strips, 1½" × 12½" (32 total)

*continued on page 9*

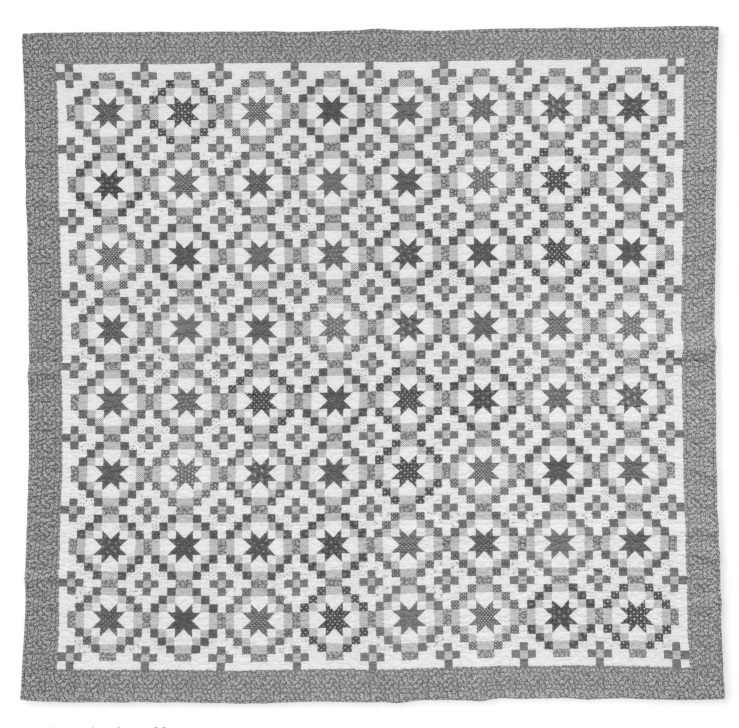

*designed and pieced by* **SUSAN ACHE**
*quilted by* **SUSAN RODGERS**

continued from page 6

From the red solid, cut:
14 strips, 1½" × 42"; crosscut 2 of the strips into
36 squares, 1½" × 1½"

From the red floral, cut:
9 strips, 4½" × 42"
15 strips, 2½" × 42"

# Making the Star Units

Press seam allowances in the directions indicated by the arrows.

**1.** Draw a diagonal line from corner to corner on the wrong side of 32 matching red print 1½" squares. Place a marked square on one end of a white 1½" × 2½" piece, right sides together. Sew on the marked line. Trim the excess corner fabric ¼" from the stitched line. Place a marked square on the opposite end of the white piece. Sew and trim as before to make a flying-geese unit measuring 1½" × 2½", including seam allowances. Make 16 sets of 16 matching units (256 total).

Make 16 sets of
16 matching units,
1½" × 2½".

**2.** Lay out four white 1½" squares, four matching flying-geese units, and one matching red print 2½" square in three rows. Sew the squares and units into rows. Join the rows to make a star unit. Make 64 units measuring 4½" square, including seam allowances.

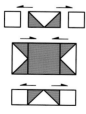 

Make 64 star units,
4½" × 4½".

# Making the Strip-Set Segments

As you cut the strip sets into segments, keep like segments together.

**1.** Sew red gingham 1½" × 12½" strips to the long sides of a white 2½" × 12½" strip to make strip set A measuring 4½" × 12½", including seam allowances. Make 16 of strip set A. Cut each strip set into eight segments, 1½" × 4½" (128 total).

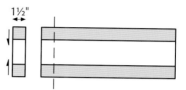

1½"

Make 16 A strip sets, 4½" × 12½".
Cut each strip into 8 segments (128 total), 1½" × 4½".

**2.** Sew matching red print 1½" × 12½" strips to the long sides of a red gingham 2½" × 12½" strip to make strip set B measuring 4½" × 12½", including seam allowances. Make 16 of strip set B. Cut each strip set into eight segments, 1½" × 4½" (128 total).

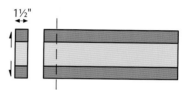

1½"

Make 16 B strip sets, 4½" × 12½".
Cut each strip into 8 segments (128 total), 1½" × 4½".

**3.** Arrange two light 1½" × 12½" strips, two matching red print 1½" × 12½" strips, two red gingham 1½" × 12½" strips, and one white 2½" × 12½" strip as shown. Sew the strips together to make strip set C measuring 8½" × 12½". Make 16 of strip set C. Cut each strip set into eight segments, 1½" × 8½" (128 total).

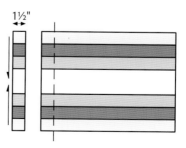

1½"

Make 16 C strip sets, 8½" × 12½".
Cut each strip into 8 segments (128 total), 1½" × 8½".

**4.** Arrange two light 2½" × 12½" strips, two matching red print 1½" × 12½" strips, and one red gingham 2½" × 12½" strip as shown. Sew the strips together to make strip set D measuring 8½" × 12½". Make 16 of strip set D. Cut each strip set into eight segments, 1½" × 8½" (128 total).

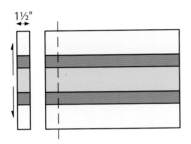

Make 16 D strip sets, 8½" × 12½".
Cut each strip into 8 segments (128 total), 1½" × 8½".

**5.** Arrange two red solid 1½" × 42" strips, two white 2½" × 42" strips, and one red floral 2½" × 42" strip as shown. Sew the strips together to make strip set E measuring 8½" × 42". Make six of strip set E. Cut the strip sets into 144 segments, 1½" × 8½". Set the segments aside to use as sashing strips.

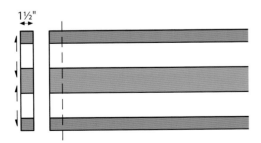

Make 6 E strip sets, 8½" × 42".
Cut 144 segments, 1½" × 8½".

## Making the Blocks

**1.** Sew the A and B segments together in pairs. Make 16 sets of eight matching units measuring 2½" × 4½", including seam allowances.

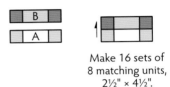

Make 16 sets of
8 matching units,
2½" × 4½".

**2.** Sew the C and D segments together in pairs. Make 16 sets of eight matching units measuring 2½" × 8½", including seam allowances.

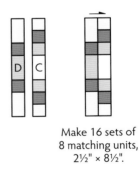

Make 16 sets of
8 matching units,
2½" × 8½".

**3.** Lay out two A/B units, two C/D units, and one star unit as shown. The red print should be the same throughout. Join the units to make a block measuring 8½" square, including seam allowances. Make 64 blocks.

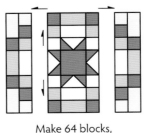

Make 64 blocks,
8½" × 8½".

# Assembling the Quilt Top

**1.** To make a sashing row, lay out nine red gingham 1½" squares and eight E segments, alternating their positions as shown. Join the pieces to make a row measuring 1½" × 73½", including seam allowances. Make nine sashing rows.

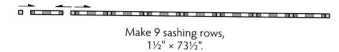

Make 9 sashing rows,
1½" × 73½".

**2.** To make a block row, lay out nine E segments and eight blocks, alternating their positions as shown. Join the pieces to make a row measuring 8½" × 73½", including seam allowances. Make eight block rows.

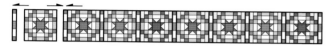

Make 8 block rows,
8½" × 73½".

**3.** Referring to the quilt assembly diagram at right, join the sashing rows and blocks rows, alternating their positions. The quilt top should measure 73½" square, including seam allowances.

**4.** To make a side inner border, join nine red solid squares and eight white 1½" × 8½" strips, alternating their positions. Make two borders measuring 1½" × 73½", including seam allowances. Make two more borders in the same way, and add a white 1½" square to each end. The top and bottom borders should measure 1½" × 75½", including seam allowances.

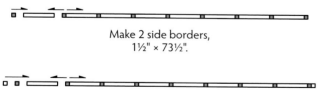

Make 2 side borders,
1½" × 73½".

Make 2 top/bottom borders,
1½" × 75½".

**5.** Sew the borders to the left and right sides and then to the top and bottom of the quilt top. The quilt top should measure 75½" square, including seam allowances.

**6.** Join the red floral 4½"-wide strips end to end. From the pieced strip, cut two 83½"-long strips and two 75½"-long strips. Sew the shorter strips to the left and right sides of the quilt center. Sew the longer strips to the top and bottom edges. The quilt top should measure 83½" square.

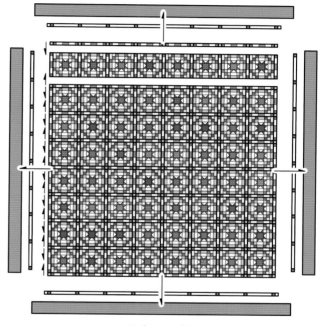

Quilt assembly

# Finishing the Quilt

For more details on any finishing steps, visit ShopMartingale.com/HowtoQuilt for free downloadable information.

**1.** Layer the quilt top with batting and backing; baste the layers together.

**2.** Quilt by hand or machine. Susan Rodgers machine quilted the quilt shown with an allover design of curved lines and loops.

**3.** Use the red floral 2½"-wide strips to make double-fold binding. Attach the binding to the quilt.

*designed and pieced by* **JESSICA DAYON**
*quilted by* **MAGGI HONEYMAN**

**5.** Lay out four red solid 2" squares, four flying-geese units, and one white 3½" square in three rows. Sew the squares and units into rows. Join the rows to make a star unit. Make 16 units measuring 6½" square, including seam allowances.

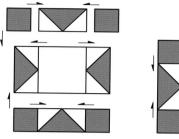 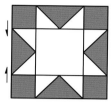

Make 16 units,
6½" × 6½".

**6.** Lay out four red solid 3½" squares, four side units, and one star unit in three rows. Sew the squares and units into rows. Join the rows to make a block measuring 12½" square, including seam allowances. Make 16 blocks.

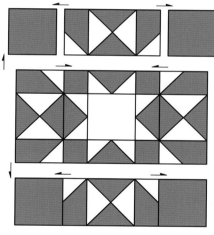

Make 16 blocks,
12½" × 12½".

## Making the Sashing Units

**1.** Draw a diagonal line from corner to corner on the wrong side of the white 1½" squares. Place marked squares on opposite corners of a red solid 2½" square. Sew on the marked lines. Trim the excess corner fabric ¼" from the stitched lines. Place marked squares on the remaining corners of the red square. Sew and trim as before to make a square-in-a-square unit measuring 2½" square, including seam allowances. Make 25 units.

Make 25 units,
2½" × 2½".

**2.** Sew B and B reversed triangles to an A triangle to make a star-point unit. Make 100 units measuring 2½" square, including seam allowances.

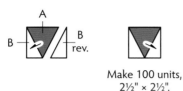

Make 100 units,
2½" × 2½".

**3.** Sew a star-point unit to each end of a red solid 2½" × 8½" strip to make a sashing strip. Make 40 strips measuring 2½" × 12½", including seam allowances.

Make 40 sashing strips,
2½" × 12½".

## Assembling the Quilt Top

Refer to the quilt assembly diagram below as needed throughout.

**1.** Join five square-in-a-square units and four sashing strips to make a sashing row. Make five rows measuring 2½" × 58½", including seam allowances.

**2.** Join five sashing strips and four blocks to make a block row. Make four rows measuring 12½" × 58½", including seam allowances.

**3.** Join the sashing rows and block rows, alternating their positions. The quilt-top center should measure 58½" square, including seam allowances.

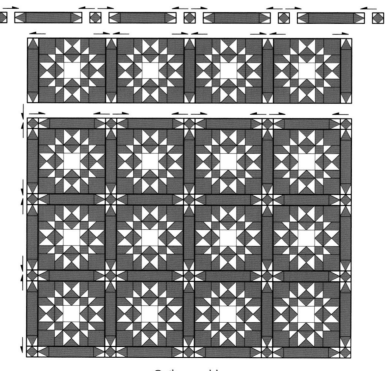

Quilt assembly

## Adding the Borders

**1.** Join five star-point units and four red solid 2½" × 12½" strips to make a side border that measures 2½" × 58½", including seam allowances. Make two. Make two more borders in the same way, and add a red 2½" square to each end. The top and bottom borders should measure 2½" × 62½", including seam allowances.

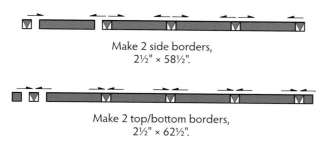

Make 2 side borders,
2½" × 58½".

Make 2 top/bottom borders,
2½" × 62½".

**2.** Sew the borders to the left and right sides of the quilt top and then to the top and bottom edges. The quilt top should measure 62½" square, including seam allowances.

**3.** Join the remaining red solid 2½"-wide strips end to end. From the pieced strip, cut two 66½"-long strips and two 62½"-long strips. Sew the shorter strips to the left and right sides of the quilt top. Sew the longer strips to the top and bottom edges. The quilt top should measure 66½" square.

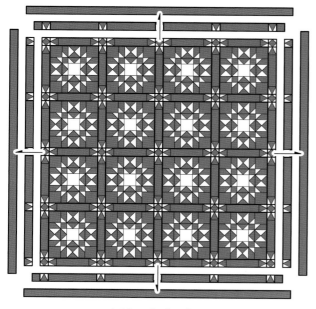

Adding the borders

## Finishing the Quilt

For more details on any finishing steps, visit ShopMartingale.com/HowtoQuilt for free downloadable information.

**1.** Layer the quilt top with batting and backing; baste the layers together.

**2.** Quilt by hand or machine. Maggi Honeyman machine quilted the quilt shown using an allover pumpkin seed design.

**3.** Use the red check 2½"-wide strips to make double-fold binding. Attach the binding to the quilt.

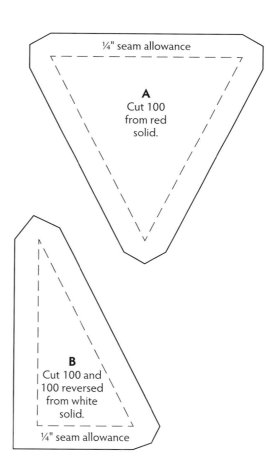

¼" seam allowance

**A**
Cut 100
from red
solid.

**B**
Cut 100 and
100 reversed
from white
solid.

¼" seam allowance

*designed and pieced by* **HELEN STUBBINGS**

*quilted by* **TRACEY BROWNING**

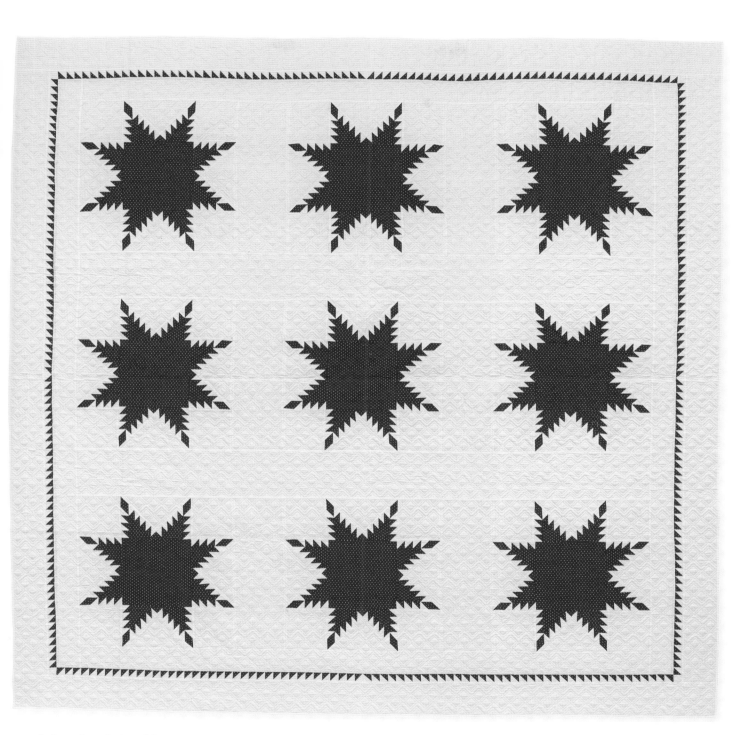

*designed and pieced by* **LISA BONGEAN**
*quilted by* **LUKE NEUBAUER OF PRIMITIVE GATHERINGS QUILT CO.**

## Adding the Borders

**1.** Sew the white 3⅜" × 71¾" strips to the top and bottom edges of the quilt top. Sew the white 3⅜" × 77½" strips to the left and right sides. The quilt top should measure 77½" square, including seam allowances.

**2.** Join 77 half-square-triangle units to make a side border, positioning 38 units to point in one direction and 39 units to point in the opposite direction. Make two borders measuring 1½" × 77½", including seam allowances. Make two more borders in the same way, and add a white 1½" square to each end. The top and bottom borders should measure 1½" × 79½", including seam allowances.

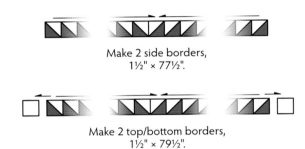

Make 2 side borders,
1½" × 77½".

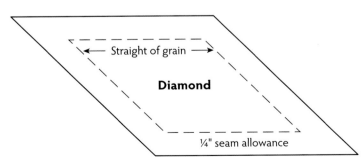

Make 2 top/bottom borders,
1½" × 79½".

**3.** Sew the borders to the left and right sides of the quilt top and then to the top and bottom edges. The quilt top should measure 79½" square, including seam allowances.

**4.** Sew the white 5½" × 79½" strips to the left and right sides of the quilt top. Sew the white 5½" × 89½" strips to the top and bottom edges. The quilt top should measure 89½" square.

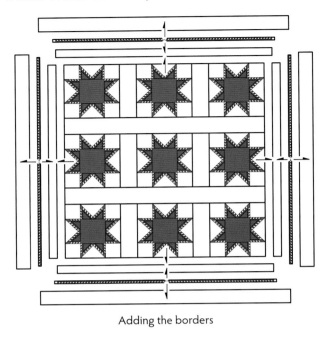

Adding the borders

## Finishing the Quilt

For more details on any finishing steps, visit ShopMartingale.com/HowtoQuilt for free downloadable information.

**1.** Layer the quilt top with batting and backing; baste the layers together.

**2.** Quilt by hand or machine. Luke Neubauer machine quilted the quilt shown with an allover double diamond design.

**3.** Use the white 2½"-wide strips to make double-fold binding. Attach the binding to the quilt.

Straight of grain

**Diamond**

¼" seam allowance

# FEATHER YOUR NEST

**DEBBIE ROBERTS**

*A delightful mix of Hens and Chickens blocks surrounded by a gentle, leafy vine is the perfect combination of patchwork and appliqué. Designer Debbie Roberts loves to mix the two techniques and especially favors the juxtaposition of the sharp edges of the patchwork against the soft curves of the appliqué motifs. Whether you display it as a wall hanging or curl up beneath it as a throw, this is a quilt you will treasure for years.*

**FINISHED QUILT: 60½" × 60½"**
**FINISHED BLOCK: 7½" × 7½" and 3" × 3"**

## Materials

*Yardage is based on 42"-wide fabric. Fat quarters measure 18" × 21".*

20 fat quarters of assorted cream prints for blocks

20 fat quarters of assorted red prints for blocks and leaf appliqués

2¼ yards of ivory tone on tone for sashing and border

1 yard of red print for vine and binding

3¾ yards of fabric for backing

67" × 67" piece of batting

¼" bias-tape maker (optional)

## Cutting

*All measurements include ¼" seam allowances.*

From *each* of 20 cream prints, cut:
2 squares, 3" × 3" (40 total)
4 pieces, 2" × 3½" (80 total)
12 squares, 2" × 2" (240 total)
4 squares, 1½" × 1½" (80 total)

From the remainder of 5 cream prints, cut:
2 squares, 2" × 2" (10 total)
4 squares, 1½" × 1½" (20 total)

*continued on page 45*

continued from page 43

From *each* of 20 red prints, cut:
2 squares, 3" × 3" (40 total)
13 squares, 2" × 2" (260 total)
1 square, 1½" × 1½" (20 total)

From the remainder of 5 red prints, cut:
2 squares, 2" × 2" (10 total)
1 square, 1½" × 1½" (5 total)
Set aside the remainder of the assorted red prints for leaf appliqués.

From the ivory tone on tone, cut on the *crosswise* grain:
3 strips, 8" × 42"; crosscut into 30 strips, 3½" × 8"

From the ivory tone on tone, cut on the *lengthwise* grain:
4 strips, 8" × 45½"
10 strips, 3½" × 8"

From the red print for vine and binding, cut:
7 strips, 2½" × 42"

From the remainder of the red print for vine and binding, cut on the bias:
½"-wide strips to total 240"

## Making the Hens and Chickens Blocks

Press seam allowances in the directions indicated by the arrows.

**1.** Draw a diagonal line from corner to corner on the wrong side of the cream 3" squares. Layer a marked square on a red 3" square, right sides together. Sew ¼" from both sides of the drawn line. Cut the unit apart on the marked line to make two half-square-triangle units. Trim the units to measure 2½" square, including seam allowances. Make 20 sets of four matching units.

Make 20 sets of
4 matching units.

**2.** Draw a diagonal line from corner to corner on the wrong side of the cream 2" squares. Layer a marked square on a red 2" square, right sides together. Sew ¼" from both sides of the drawn line. Cut the unit apart on the marked line to make two half-square-triangle units. Trim the units to 1½" square, including seam allowances. Make 20 sets of 20 matching units and 25 sets of four matching units (500 total). Set aside the 25 sets of four matching units for the Shoo Fly blocks.

Make 500 units.

**3.** Lay out five small triangle units from step 2 and one large triangle unit from step 1 as shown. Join the small units into rows. Sew the rows to the large unit to make a corner unit measuring 3½" square, including seam allowances. Make 20 sets of four matching units.

Make 20 sets of
4 matching units,
3½" × 3½".

**4.** Lay out four matching corner units, four cream 2" × 3½" pieces, and one red 2" square in three rows. The cream and red prints should be the same throughout. Sew the pieces into rows. Join the rows to make a block measuring 8" square, including seam allowances. Make 20 Hens and Chickens blocks.

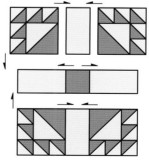

Make 20 Hens and Chickens blocks,
8" × 8".

## Making the Shoo Fly Blocks

Lay out four of the small half-square-triangle units that you set aside earlier, four cream 1½" squares, and one red 1½" square in three rows. The cream and red prints should be the same throughout. Sew the pieces into rows. Join the rows to make a block measuring 3½" square, including seam allowances. Make 25 Shoo Fly blocks.

Make 25 Shoo Fly blocks,
3½" × 3½".

## Assembling the Quilt Top

Refer to the quilt assembly diagram on page 47 as needed throughout.

**1.** Join five Shoo Fly blocks and four ivory 3½" × 8" strips, alternating their positions, to make a sashing row. Make five rows measuring 3½" × 45½", including seam allowances.

**2.** Join four Hens and Chickens blocks and five ivory 3½" × 8" strips, alternating their positions, to make a block row. Make four rows measuring 8" × 45½", including seam allowances. You'll have four blocks left over for the outer border.

**3.** Join the sashing rows and block rows, alternating their positions. The quilt top should measure 45½" square, including seam allowances.

## Making and Adding the Appliquéd Border

For more information on appliqué techniques, go to ShopMartingale.com/HowtoQuilt.

**1.** Sew the red ½"-wide strips together end to end. Cut four ½" × 60" strips. Press under ¼" on the long edges (or use a ¼" bias-tape maker) to prepare the red vines for appliqué. Debbie used turned-edge appliqué.

**2.** Using the patterns on page 49, prepare 12 oak leaves, 32 large leaves, and 16 small leaves for appliqué.

**3.** Fold each ivory 8" × 45½" strip in half widthwise to mark the center; unfold. Referring to the diagram below and the photo on page 48, position and appliqué one vine, three oak leaves, eight large leaves, and four small leaves on an ivory strip. Trim the ends of the vine even with the edges of the ivory strip. Repeat to make four borders measuring 8" × 45½", including seam allowances.

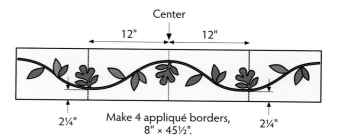

Make 4 appliqué borders, 8" × 45½".

Quilt assembly

*Pieced and quilted by* **DEBBIE ROBERTS**

**4.** Sew appliquéd borders to the left and right sides of the quilt top. Sew a Hens and Chickens block to each end of the two remaining appliquéd borders. Sew these borders to the top and bottom edges. The quilt top should measure 60½" square.

Adding the borders

# Finishing the Quilt

For more details on any finishing steps, visit ShopMartingale.com/HowtoQuilt for free downloadable information.

**1.** Layer the quilt top with batting and backing; baste the layers together.

**2.** Quilt by hand or machine. Debbie Roberts machine quilted the quilt shown with an allover feather and swirl motif.

**3.** Use the red 2½"-wide strips to make double-fold binding. Attach the binding to the quilt.

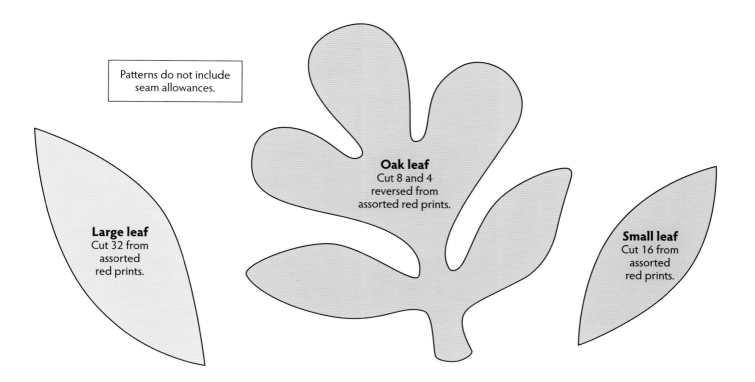

Patterns do not include
seam allowances.

**Large leaf**
Cut 32 from
assorted
red prints.

**Oak leaf**
Cut 8 and 4
reversed from
assorted red prints.

**Small leaf**
Cut 16 from
assorted
red prints.

# OH, MY STARS!

•••••

## FROM THE COLLECTION OF JENNIFER KELTNER

*Hidden away in the back room of an antique shop, a vintage red-and-white quilt top was just waiting to be discovered and loved. After patching a few torn hand-sewn seams, Jennifer had this fabulous find machine quilted with a Baptist fan pattern, in keeping with the traditions from its era. While the stars are what pop in the design, the block is actually a simple Nine Patch and the stars don't appear until the sashing is added.*

**FINISHED QUILT: 72½" × 81½"**
**FINISHED BLOCK: 6" × 6"**

## Materials

*Yardage is based on 42"-wide fabric.*

4⅝ yards of ivory solid for patchwork

5⅞ yards of red solid for patchwork and binding

6¾ yards of fabric for backing (**Note:** if your backing fabric is at least 41" wide after removing the selvages, you will need only 5 yards.)

81" × 90" piece of batting

## Cutting

*All measurements include ¼" seam allowances.*

### From the ivory solid, cut:
22 strips, 3½" × 42"; crosscut into 127 pieces, 3½" × 6½"

25 strips, 2½" × 42"

6 strips, 2" × 42"; crosscut into 34 strips, 2" × 6½"

### From the red solid, cut:
6 strips, 3½" × 42"; crosscut into 56 squares, 3½" × 3½"

62 strips, 2½" × 42"; crosscut *34 of the strips* into 508 squares, 2½" × 2½"

8 strips, 2" × 42"; crosscut into:

      30 pieces, 2" × 3½"

      68 pieces, 2" × 2½"

      4 squares, 2" × 2"

*antique quilt from the collection of* **JENNIFER KELTNER**
*quilted by* **MAGGI HONEYMAN**

# Making the Blocks

Press seam allowances in the directions indicated by the arrows.

**1.** Sew an ivory strip to each long side of a red 2½"-wide strip to make strip set A measuring 6½" × 42", including seam allowances. Make 10 of strip set A. Cut the strip sets into 144 segments, 2½" × 6½".

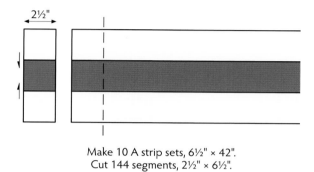

Make 10 A strip sets, 6½" × 42".
Cut 144 segments, 2½" × 6½".

**2.** Sew a red 2½"-wide strip to each long side of an ivory strip to make strip set B measuring 6½" × 42", including seam allowances. Make five of strip set B. Cut the strip sets into 72 segments, 2½" × 6½".

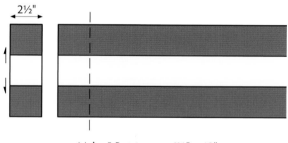

Make 5 B strip sets, 6½" × 42".
Cut 72 segments, 2½" × 6½".

**3.** Join two A segments and one B segment to make a Nine Patch block measuring 6½" square, including seam allowances. Make 72 blocks.

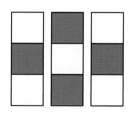 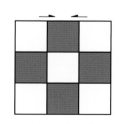

Make 72 blocks,
6½" × 6½".

# Making the Star Sashing

**1.** Draw a diagonal line from corner to corner on the wrong side of the red 2½" squares. Position a marked square on one corner of an ivory 3½" × 6½" piece. Sew on the marked line. Trim the excess corner fabric ¼" from the stitched line. In the same way, sew marked squares on the remaining three corners of the ivory piece to make a star unit measuring 3½" × 6½", including seam allowances. Make 127 units.

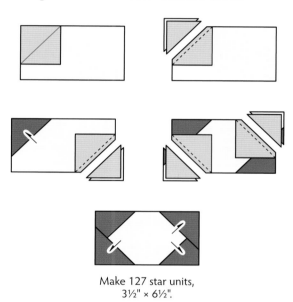

Make 127 star units,
3½" × 6½".

**2.** On the wrong side of 34 red 2" × 2½" pieces, align the 45° line of a square ruler with a long edge of the piece and draw a diagonal line from the top corner to the bottom edge. **Note:** Do not draw from corner to corner. Draw a line in the opposite direction on the remaining 34 red 2" × 2½" pieces.

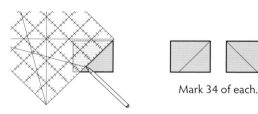

Mark 34 of each.

**3.** Making the half stars around the perimeter of the quilt requires half sashing units. Layer a marked red piece on top of a white 2" × 6½" strip, aligning the corners. Sew on the marked line. Trim the excess corner fabric ¼" from the stitched line. Repeat to sew a marked red piece to the other end of the white strip, noting the orientation of the marked line. Make 34 half-star units measuring 2" × 6½", including seam allowances.

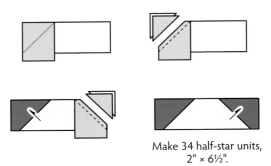

Make 34 half-star units,
2" × 6½".

## Assembling the Quilt Top

**1.** To make a block row, lay out eight blocks and seven star units, alternating their positions as shown. Place a half-star unit at the beginning and end of the row. Join the blocks and units to make a row measuring 6½" × 72½", including seam allowances. Make nine block rows.

Make 9 block rows,
6½" × 72½".

**2.** To make a sashing row, lay out eight star units and seven red 3½" squares, alternating their positions as shown. Place a red 2" × 3½" piece at the beginning and end of the row. Join the pieces to make a row measuring 3½" × 72½", including seam allowances. Make eight sashing rows.

Make 8 sashing rows,
3½" × 72½".

**3.** To make the top sashing row that completes the star design, lay out eight half-star units and seven red 2" × 3½" pieces as shown. Place a red 2" square at each end of the row. Join the pieces to make a row measuring 2" × 72½", including seam allowances. Repeat to make the bottom row.

Make 2 top/bottom rows,
2" × 72½".

**4.** Referring to the quilt assembly diagram below, lay out the block rows, alternating them with the sashing rows from step 2. Add the top and bottom sashing rows to the layout, and then join the rows. The quilt top should measure 72½" × 81½".

## Finishing the Quilt

For more details on any finishing steps, visit ShopMartingale.com/HowtoQuilt for free downloadable information.

**1.** Layer the quilt top with batting and backing; baste the layers together.

**2.** Quilt by hand or machine. Maggi Honeyman machine quilted the quilt shown using a Baptist fan pattern.

**3.** Use the remaining red 2½"-wide strips to make double-fold binding. Attach the binding to the quilt.

Quilt assembly

# DOUBLE TAKE

**LISSA ALEXANDER**

*Double Hour Glass blocks do double duty creating a secondary design when combined with skinny sashing and cornerstones on designer Lissa Alexander's red-and-white beauty. Looking for a vintage feel, Lissa chose a red pin dot fabric for the blocks instead of using solid red. Wanting a make-do feel, she purposely selected a different scale of red dot for the binding. And then, an "oops" happened! Lissa didn't have enough of her chosen fabric to make binding for the entire quilt, so the binding is pieced from two different fabrics. She loves the charm and imperfection of the binding even more.*

**FINISHED QUILT: 75" × 90"**
**FINISHED BLOCK: 13½" × 13½"**

## Materials

*Yardage is based on 42"-wide fabric.*

6⅝ yards of white solid for blocks, sashing, and borders

3½ yards of red dot for blocks, sashing, inner border, and binding*

7 yards of fabric for backing

83" × 98" piece of batting

*\*If you wish to use two fabrics for the binding, you'll need ⅓ yard of a different red print.*

### Triangle Papers

*If you wish to use your favorite brand of triangle paper, do not cut the 2½" squares from the white solid and red dot. Instead, skip step 1 of "Making the Blocks" below and follow the directions on the package. You'll need triangle papers that finish at 2".*

## Cutting

*All measurements include ¼" seam allowances.*

From the white solid, cut on the *crosswise* grain:
9 strips, 5⅜" × 42"; crosscut into 60 squares, 5⅜" × 5⅜". Cut the squares in half diagonally to yield 120 triangles.

5 strips, 5" × 42"; crosscut into 40 squares, 5" × 5"

13 strips, 2½" × 42"; crosscut into 182 squares, 2½" × 2½"

14 strips, 2" × 42"; crosscut into:
  27 strips, 2" × 14"
  22 squares, 2" × 2"

*continued on page 59*

designed and pieced by **LISSA ALEXANDER**
quilted by **MAGGI HONEYMAN**

*continued from page 57*

**From the white solid, cut on the *lengthwise* grain:**
2 strips, 5½" × 80"
2 strips, 5½" × 75"
40 strips, 2" × 14"

**From the red dot, cut:**
3 strips, 5" × 42"; crosscut into 20 squares, 5" × 5"
13 strips, 2½" × 42"; crosscut into 182 squares,
 2½" × 2½"
12 strips, 2⅜" × 42"; crosscut into 180 squares,
 2⅜" × 2⅜". Cut the squares in half diagonally to yield
 360 triangles.
8 strips, 2" × 42"; crosscut into 146 squares, 2" × 2"
9 strips, 2½" × 42"

## Making the Blocks

Press seam allowances in the directions indicated by the arrows.

**1.** Draw a diagonal line from corner to corner on the wrong side of the white 2½" squares. Layer a marked square on a red 2½" square, right sides together. Sew ¼" from both sides of the drawn line. Cut the unit apart on the marked line to make two half-square-triangle units. Trim the units to measure 2" square, including seam allowances. Make 364 units.

Make 364 units.

**2.** Lay out three red triangles and three half-square-triangle units in three rows as shown. Sew the pieces into rows. Join the rows to make a triangle unit. Make 120 units. Set aside the remaining half-square-triangle units for the inner border.

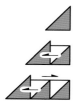

Make 120 units.

**3.** Sew a white triangle to the long side of each unit from step 2. Make 120 A units measuring 5" square, including seam allowances.

Make 120 A units,
5" × 5".

**4.** Draw a diagonal line from corner to corner on the wrong side of 80 red 2" squares. Place a marked square on the white corner of an A unit, right sides together. Sew on the marked line. Trim the excess corner fabric ¼" from the stitched line. Make 40 B units measuring 5" square, including seam allowances.

Make 40 B units,
5" × 5".

**5.** Place a marked red square from step 4 on one corner of a white 5" square, right sides together. Sew on the marked line. Trim the excess corner fabric ¼" from the stitched line. Make 40 C units measuring 5" square, including seam allowances.

Make 40 C units,
5" × 5".

**6.** Lay out four A units, two B units, two C units, and one red 5" square in three rows. Sew the units and square into rows. Join the rows to make a block measuring 14" square, including seam allowances. Make 20 blocks.

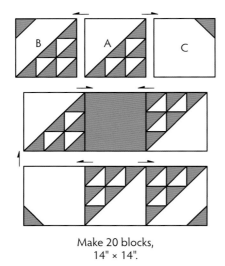

Make 20 blocks,
14" × 14".

## Assembling the Quilt Top

Refer to the quilt assembly diagram at right as needed throughout.

**1.** Join five red 2" squares and four white 2" × 14" strips to make a sashing row. Make six sashing rows measuring 2" × 62", including seam allowances.

**2.** Join five white 2" × 14" strips and four blocks, rotating every other block to make a block row. Make five block rows measuring 14" × 62", including seam allowances.

**3.** Join the sashing rows and block rows, alternating their positions and rotating every other block row as shown. The quilt top should measure 62" × 77", including seam allowances.

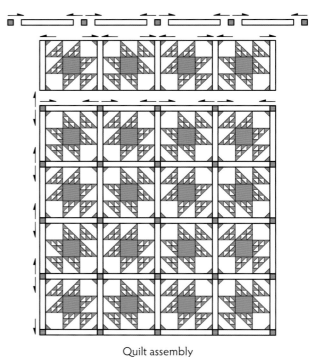

Quilt assembly

## Adding the Borders

**1.** Draw a diagonal line from corner to corner on the wrong side of the remaining red 2" squares. Place a marked square on each end of a white 2" × 14" strip, right sides together. Sew on the marked line. Trim the excess corner fabric ¼" from the stitched line. Make 18 border units measuring 2" × 14", including seam allowances.

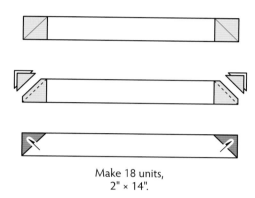

Make 18 units,
2" × 14".

**2.** Join five border units and six white 2" squares to make a side border measuring 2" × 77", including seam allowances. Make two side borders. Join four border units, five white 2" squares, and two half-square-triangle units to make a top border measuring 2" × 65", including seam allowances. Repeat to make the bottom border.

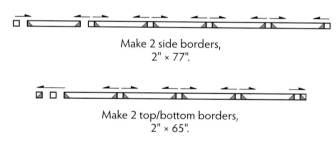

Make 2 side borders,
2" × 77".

Make 2 top/bottom borders,
2" × 65".

**3.** Referring to the diagram at right, sew the borders to the left and right sides of the quilt top and then to the top and bottom edges. The quilt top should measure 65" × 80", including seam allowances.

**4.** Sew the white 5½" × 80" strips to the left and right sides of the quilt top. Sew the white 5½" × 75" strips to the top and bottom edges. The quilt top should measure 75" × 90".

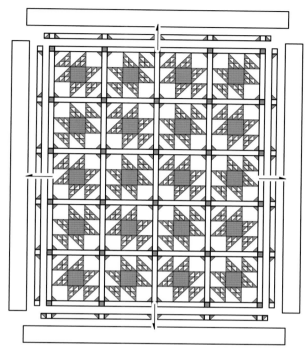

Adding the borders

## Finishing the Quilt

For more details on any finishing steps, visit ShopMartingale.com/HowtoQuilt for free downloadable information.

**1.** Layer the quilt top with batting and backing; baste the layers together.

**2.** Quilt by hand or machine. Maggi Honeyman machine quilted the quilt shown using a feathered wreath motif and a diagonal crosshatch grid in the center of each block. A larger feathered wreath and grid is stitched where the blocks and sashing form a Shoo Fly block. Curved lines are stitched in the red and white small triangles. A pumpkin seed design is stitched between the wreaths and a diagonal crosshatch grid is stitched in the outer border.

**3.** Use the red 2½"-wide strips to make double-fold binding. Attach the binding to the quilt.

# THIS AND THAT

## NANCY MARTIN

Red and white is right in the wheelhouse of designer Nancy Martin, who's been collecting fabrics, quilts, and home decor in the signature palette for years. Her quilt features a melange of red prints mingled with creamy lights. The pattern that emerges may depend on your point of view. Is it faceted jewels, little bow ties, or spinning pinwheels? It might just be a bit of this and a little of that.

**FINISHED QUILT: 59½" × 74½"**
**FINISHED BLOCK: 5" × 11"**

## Materials

*Yardage is based on 42"-wide fabric.*

3¼ yards *total* of assorted light prints for blocks and pieced borders

2½ yards *total* of assorted red prints for blocks and triangle border

⅓ yard of light print for border 3

1½ yards of red print for outer border and binding*

4½ yards of fabric for backing

66" × 81" piece of batting

*Nancy finished her quilt with bias binding. If you'd like to do the same, you'll need 2 yards of the red print for outer border and binding.*

## Cutting

*All measurements include ¼" seam allowances.*

**From the assorted light prints, cut a *total* of:**
40 sets of 2 *matching* pieces, 3" × 6" (80 total)
20 assorted pieces, 3" × 6"
16 pieces, 3" × 5½"
42 squares, 3½" × 3½"
40 sets of 2 *matching* squares, 3" × 3" (80 total)
8 assorted squares, 3" × 3"

**From the assorted red prints, cut a *total* of:**
40 sets of 2 *matching* pieces, 3" × 6" (80 total)
42 squares, 3½" × 3½"
40 sets of 2 *matching* squares, 3" × 3" (80 total)

**From the light print for border 3, cut:**
6 strips, 1½" × 42"

**From the red print for outer border and binding, cut:**
7 strips, 4" × 42"
7 strips, 2½" × 42"

## Making the Blocks

Press seam allowances in the directions indicated by the arrows. For each block, use matching sets of two red 3" × 6" pieces and two 3" cream squares. Likewise, choose two matching cream rectangles and two matching red squares.

**1.** Draw a diagonal line from corner to corner on the wrong side of the red 3" squares. Place a marked square on one end of a light 3" × 6" piece, right sides together. Sew on the marked line. Trim the excess corner fabric ¼" from the stitched line. Make 80 A units measuring 3" × 6", including seam allowances.

Make 80 A units,
3" × 6".

**2.** Draw a diagonal line from corner to corner on the wrong side of 80 light 3" squares. Place a marked square on one end of a red 3" × 6" piece, right sides together. Sew on the marked line. Trim the excess corner fabric ¼" from the stitched line. Make 80 B units measuring 3" × 6", including seam allowances.

Make 80 B units,
3" × 6".

**3.** Lay out two matching A and two matching B units in two rows, rotating the units in the bottom row as shown. Sew the units into rows. Join the rows to make a block measuring 5½" × 11½", including seam allowances. Make 40 blocks.

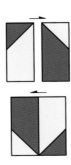 

Make 40 blocks,
5½" × 11½".

## Assembling the Quilt Top

Lay out the blocks in five rows of eight blocks each as shown in the quilt assembly diagram below. Sew the blocks into rows and then join the rows. The quilt top should measure 40½" × 55½", including seam allowances.

## Adding the Borders

Refer to the adding the borders diagram on page 67 as needed throughout.

**1.** Join 10 light 3" × 6" pieces to make a side border measuring 3" × 55½", including seam allowances. Make two. Join two light 3" squares and eight light 3" × 5½" pieces to make a top border measuring

3" × 45½", including seam allowances. Repeat to make the bottom border.

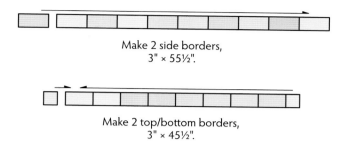

Make 2 side borders,
3" × 55½".

Make 2 top/bottom borders,
3" × 45½".

**2.** Sew the borders to the left and right sides of the quilt top and then to the top and bottom edges. The quilt top should measure 45½" × 60½", including seam allowances.

Quilt assembly

designed and pieced by **NANCY MARTIN**
quilted by **SHELLY NOLTE**

**3.** Draw a diagonal line from corner to corner on the wrong side of the light 3½" squares. Layer a marked square on a red 3½" square, right sides together. Sew ¼" from both sides of the drawn line. Cut the unit apart on the marked line to make two half-square-triangle units. Trim the units to measure 3" square, including seam allowances. Make 84 units.

Make 84 units.

**4.** Join 24 half-square-triangle units to make a side border that measures 3" × 60½", including seam allowances. Make two. Join 18 half-square-triangle units, and add a light 3" square to each end to make a top border measuring 3" × 50½", including seam allowances. Repeat to make the bottom border.

Make 2 side borders,
3" × 60½".

Make 2 top/bottom borders,
3" × 50½".

**5.** Sew the triangle borders to the left and right sides of the quilt top and then to the top and bottom. The quilt top should measure 50½" × 65½", including seam allowances.

**6.** Join the light 1½"-wide strips end to end. From the pieced strip, cut two 65½"-long strips and two 52½"-long strips. Sew the longer strips to the left and right sides of the quilt top. Sew the shorter strips to the top and bottom edges. The quilt top should measure 52½" × 67½", including seam allowances.

### Start with Diagonal Ends

*To make the 1½"-wide border, Nancy sewed the strips together using diagonal seams. For ease in sewing, she used a rotary cutter and ruler with a 45° line to cut the ends at an angle.*

**7.** Join the red 4"-wide strips end to end. From the pieced strip, cut two 67½"-long strips and two 59½"-long strips. Sew the longer strips to the left and right sides of the quilt top. Sew the shorter strips to the top and bottom edges. The quilt top should measure 59½" × 74½".

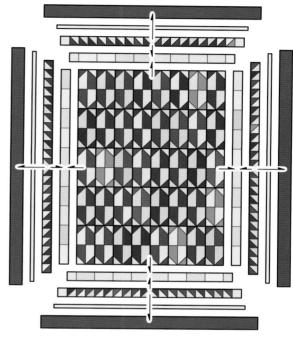

Adding the borders

## Finishing the Quilt

For more details on any finishing steps, visit ShopMartingale.com/HowtoQuilt for free downloadable information.

**1.** Layer the quilt top with batting and backing; baste the layers together.

**2.** Quilt by hand or machine. Shelly Nolte machine quilted the quilt shown with an allover large swirl design.

**3.** Use the red 2½"-wide strips to make double-fold binding. Attach the binding to the quilt.

**3.** Lay out four red solid 2½" squares, four flying-geese units, and one center unit in three rows as shown. Sew the squares and units into rows. Join the rows to make a star unit measuring 8½" square, including seam allowances. Make 13 units.

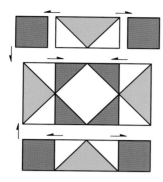

Make 13 star units,
8½" × 8½".

**4.** Draw a diagonal line from corner to corner on the wrong side of the remaining red solid 2½" squares. Place marked squares on opposite ends of a white 2½" × 8½" piece. Sew on the marked lines. Trim the excess corner fabric ¼" from the stitched lines. Make 52 side units measuring 2½" × 8½", including seam allowances.

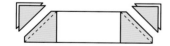

Make 52 side units,
2½" × 8½".

**5.** Lay out four white 2½" squares, four side units, and one star unit in three rows as shown. Sew the squares and units into rows. Join the rows to make a block measuring 12½" square, including seam allowances. Make 13 Double Star blocks.

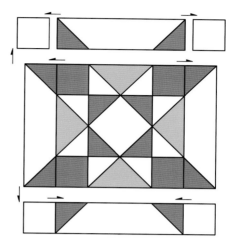

Make 13 Double Star blocks,
12½" × 12½".

## Making the Variable Star Blocks

**1.** Draw a diagonal line from corner to corner on the wrong side of 64 red solid 3½" squares. Place a marked square on one end of a white 3½" × 6½" piece, right sides together. Sew on the marked line. Trim the excess corner fabric ¼" from the stitched line. Place a marked square on the opposite end of the white piece. Sew and trim as before to make a flying-geese unit measuring 3½" × 6½", including seam allowances. Make 32 units.

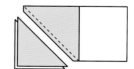

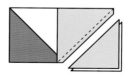
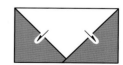

Make 32 units,
3½" × 6½".

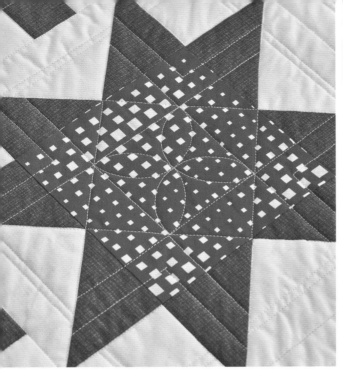

**2.** Lay out four white 3½" squares, four flying-geese units, and one red dot square as shown. Sew the squares and units into rows. Join the rows to make a block measuring 12½" square, including seam allowances. Make eight Variable Star blocks.

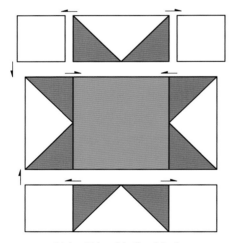

Make 8 Variable Star blocks,
12½" × 12½".

## Making the Checkerboard Blocks

**1.** Lay out eight white and eight red solid 2" squares in four rows of four squares each. Sew the squares into rows. Join the rows to make a 16-patch center unit. Make four units measuring 6½" square, including seam allowances.

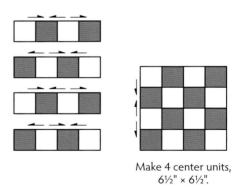

Make 4 center units,
6½" × 6½".

**2.** Join two red solid and two white 2" × 3½" pieces, alternating their positions to make a side unit. Make 16 units measuring 3½" × 6½", including seam allowances.

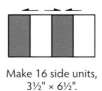

Make 16 side units,
3½" × 6½".

# TRIBUTE

· · · · ·

## SHERRI MCCONNELL

*Joanna S. Rose's 2011 exhibition of 650 red-and-white quilts in the Park Avenue Armory in New York City inspired designer Sherri McConnell to create her own red-and-white pattern as a tribute to that show. That exhibit, plus a smaller iteration that later hung on display in Houston at International Quilt Market, motivated Sherri to create several red-and-white quilts herself to begin her own collection of classic two-color quilts.*

**FINISHED QUILT: 51½" × 51½"**
**FINISHED BLOCK: 8" × 8"**

## Materials

*Yardage is based on 42"-wide fabric. Fat eighths measure 9" × 21".*

13 fat eighths of assorted coral prints for blocks

2⅞ yards of white solid for blocks, sashing, and border

1 fat eighth of coral check for sashing

½ yard of coral dot for binding

3¼ yards of fabric for backing

58" × 58" piece of batting

## Cutting

*As you cut, keep like prints together. All measurements include ¼" seam allowances.*

From *each* of 12 assorted coral prints, cut:
2 strips, 3" × 21"; crosscut into 12 squares, 3" × 3" (144 total)

From the remaining coral print fat eighth, cut:
1 strip, 3" × 21"; crosscut into 6 squares, 3" × 3"

From the white solid, cut:
6 strips, 4" × 42"
12 strips, 3" × 42"; crosscut into 150 squares, 3" × 3"
7 strips, 2½" × 42"; crosscut into 100 squares, 2½" × 2½"
10 strips, 1½" × 42"; crosscut into 40 strips, 1½" × 8½"

From the coral check, cut:
2 strips, 1½" × 21"; crosscut into 16 squares, 1½" × 1½"

From the coral dot, cut:
6 strips, 2½" × 42"

*designed and pieced by* **SHERRI MCCONNELL**
*quilted by* **MARIAN BOTT**

## Making the Blocks

Press seam allowances in the directions indicated by the arrows.

**1.** Draw a diagonal line from corner to corner on the wrong side of the white 3" squares. Layer a marked square on a coral print 3" square, right sides together. Sew ¼" from both sides of the drawn line. Cut the unit apart on the marked line to make two half-square-triangle units. Trim the units to measure 2½" square, including seam allowances. Make 300 units.

Make 300 units.

**2.** Lay out 12 half-square-triangle units and four white 2½" squares in four rows. Notice, in the photo on page 84, that in some blocks Sherri used one set of eight matching units and one set of four matching units. In other blocks she used two sets of six matching units each. Sew the pieces into rows and then join the rows to make block A. Make 23 blocks measuring 8½" square, including seam allowances.

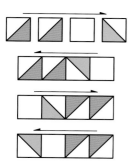 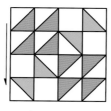

Make 23 A blocks,
8½" × 8½".

**3.** Lay out 12 half-square-triangle units and four white 2½" squares in four rows, noting the orientation of the units in the lower-left corner. Sew the pieces into rows and then join the rows to make block B. Make two blocks measuring 8½" square, including seam allowances.

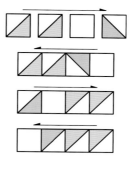 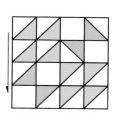

Make 2 B blocks,
8½" × 8½".

## Assembling the Quilt Top

Refer to the quilt assembly diagram on page 86 as needed throughout.

**1.** Join five blocks and four white 1½" × 8½" strips to make a block row. Make five rows measuring 8½" × 44½", including seam allowances.

**2.** Join five white 1½" × 8½" strips and four coral check squares to make a sashing row. Make four rows measuring 1½" × 44½", including seam allowances.

**3.** Join the block rows and sashing rows, alternating their positions. The quilt top should measure 44½" square, including seam allowances.

**4.** Join the white 4"-wide strips end to end. From the pieced strip, cut two 51½"-long strips and two 44½"-long strips. Sew the shorter strips to the left and right sides of the quilt center. Sew the longer strips to the top and bottom edges. The quilt top should measure 51½" square.

## Finishing the Quilt

For more details on any finishing steps, visit ShopMartingale.com/HowtoQuilt for free downloadable information.

**1.** Layer the quilt top with batting and backing; baste the layers together.

**2.** Quilt by hand or machine. Marian Bott machine quilted the quilt shown with an allover swirl design.

**3.** Use the coral dot 2½"-wide strips to make double-fold binding. Attach the binding to the quilt.

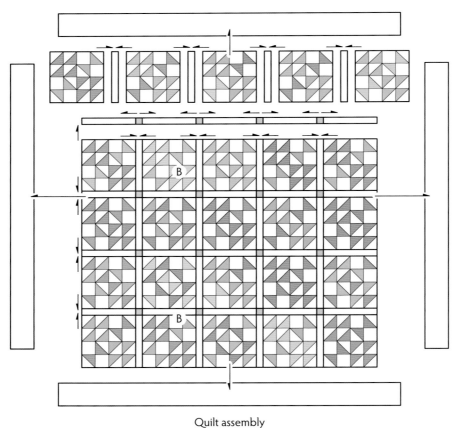

Quilt assembly

# SIMPLY RED

## KAREN STYLES

*Medallion-style quilts with their center motifs surrounded by a series of borders were quite popular in the early 1800s. Aussie designer Karen Styles put her own spin on the style with a trio of stars. Worried that your piecing might not be spot on enough to make it all fit together precisely? Fear not! Border strips between rounds allow for minor adjustments as you go, resulting in a spectacular finish that shines with beauty.*

**FINISHED QUILT: 67½" × 67½"**
**FINISHED BLOCK: 30" × 30" AND 6" × 6"**

## Materials

*Yardage is based on 42"-wide fabric.*

½ yard of red print A for center Star block

¼ yard of red print B for center Star block

½ yard of ecru print for blocks

5 yards of cream print for blocks and borders

2½ yards *total* of assorted red prints for blocks and borders

⅝ yard of red check for binding

4⅛ yards of fabric for backing

74" × 74" piece of batting

## Cutting

*All measurements include ¼" seam allowances. You may wish to cut the cream print border strips later, adjusting the width or length slightly to allow for sewing differences.*

**From red print A, cut:**
5 strips, 2½" × 42"

**From red print B, cut:**
2 strips, 2½" × 42"

*continued on page 89*

*continued from page 87*

**From the ecru print, cut:**

3 strips, 3½" × 42"; crosscut into 28 squares, 3½" × 3½"

2 strips, 2½" × 42"

**From the cream print, cut:**

1 strip, 13¾" × 42"; crosscut into 1 square,
   13¾" × 13¾". Cut the square into quarters diagonally
   to yield 4 large triangles.

2 strips, 4" × 42"; crosscut into:
      4 pieces, 4" × 8"
      4 pieces, 4" × 4½"

9 strips, 3⅛" × 42"; crosscut into 108 squares,
   3⅛" × 3⅛". Cut the squares into quarters diagonally
   to yield 432 small triangles.

7 strips, 3" × 42"

17 strips, 2" × 42"; crosscut into:
      112 pieces, 2" × 3½"
      112 squares, 2" × 2"

13 strips, 1¾" × 42"; crosscut *4 of the strips* into:
      4 strips, 1¾" × 9¼"
      4 strips, 1¾" × 8"
      40 squares, 1¾" × 1¾"

17 strips, 1½" × 42"; crosscut *8 of the strips* into:
      2 strips, 1½" × 39½"
      2 strips, 1½" × 32½"
      2 strips, 1½" × 30½"
      16 pieces, 1½" × 2½"
      16 squares, 1½" × 1½"

4 strips, 1¼" × 42"; crosscut into 20 strips, 1¼" × 6½"

2 strips, 1⅛" × 42"; crosscut into 8 strips, 1⅛" × 6½"

**From 1 of the assorted red prints, cut:**

4 squares, 2½" × 2½"

32 squares, 1½" × 1½"

**From the assorted red prints, cut a *total* of:**

22 strips, 1¾" × 42"; crosscut *13 of the strips* into:
      27 strips, 1¾" × 13¼"
      80 squares, 1¾" × 1¾"

28 sets of 8 squares, 2" × 2" (224 total)

28 sets of 4 squares, 1½" × 1½" (112 total)

**From the red check, cut:**

7 strips, 2½" × 42"

## Making the Star-Point Units

Press seam allowances in the directions indicated by the arrows.

**1.** Sew a red A strip to each long side of a red B strip to make a strip set measuring 6½" × 42", including seam allowances. Position a ruler so that the 45° diagonal marking is aligned with a seamline, and trim the left end of the strip set.

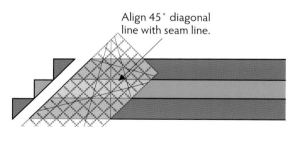

Align 45° diagonal line with seam line.

Make 1 A strip set,
6½" × 42".

**2.** Position the ruler so that the 45° diagonal marking aligns with the seamline and the 2½" measurement is even with the angled edge of the strip set. Cut eight 2½"-wide A segments.

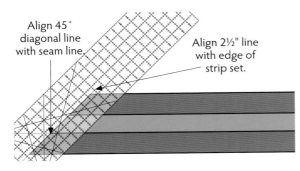

Align 45° diagonal line with seam line.

Align 2½" line with edge of strip set.

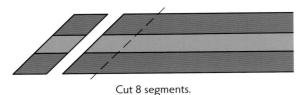

Cut 8 segments.

**3.** Repeat steps 1 and 2, using one red B strip, one red A strip, and one ecru 2½"-wide strip to make strip set B. Cut eight 2½"-wide B segments.

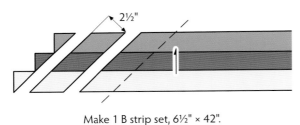

2½"

Make 1 B strip set, 6½" × 42".
Cut 8 segments.

**4.** Repeat steps 1 and 2, using two red A strips and one ecru 2½"-wide strip to make strip set C. Cut eight 2½"-wide C segments.

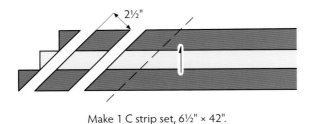

2½"

Make 1 C strip set, 6½" × 42".
Cut 8 segments.

**5.** Place an A segment on top of a B segment, right sides together. Offset the point at the top edge ¼" as shown. Sew the segments together. In the same way, sew a C segment to the opposite side of the B segment to make a diamond unit. Make eight units.

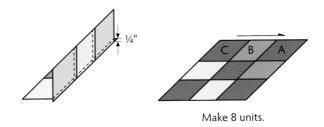

¼"

C B A

Make 8 units.

**6.** On the wrong side of each unit, mark opposite corners ¼" from the raw edge in preparation for Y-seam construction. On the wrong side of each cream large triangle, mark the right-angle corner ¼" from the raw edge.

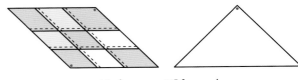

Mark corners ¼" from edge.

**7.** Lay out two diamond units and one cream large triangle as shown. Place the diamond units right sides together and, starting with a backstitch, sew from the ¼" mark to the diamond tip. Place the cream triangle on top of one diamond unit, right sides together and matching the ¼" marks. Starting with a backstitch at the ¼" mark, sew to the outside edge. Pivot the cream triangle so the other short edge is along the second diamond unit.

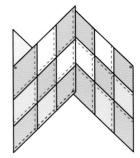

**8.** In the same way, sew the triangle to the second diamond unit, starting at the 1/4" mark and sewing to the outside edge. Repeat the process to make four units.

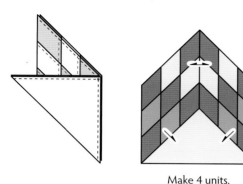

Make 4 units.

## Completing the Center Star

**1.** Draw a diagonal line from corner to corner on the wrong side of 32 matching red 1½" squares. Place a marked square on one end of a cream 1½" × 2½" piece, right sides together. Sew on the marked line. Trim the excess corner fabric ¼" from the stitched line. Place a marked square on the opposite end of the cream piece. Sew and trim as before to make a flying-geese unit measuring 1½" × 2½". Make 16 units.

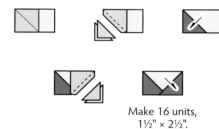

Make 16 units,
1½" × 2½".

**2.** Lay out four cream 1½" squares, four flying-geese units, and one matching red 2½" square in three rows. Sew the squares and units into rows. Join the rows to make a star unit measuring 4½" square, including seam allowances. Make four identical units.

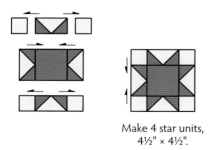

Make 4 star units,
4½" × 4½".

**3.** Sew a cream 4" × 4½" piece to the right side of a star unit from step 2. Sew a cream 4" × 8" piece to the bottom edge. Sew a cream 1¾" × 8" strip to the left side and a cream 1¾" × 9¼" strip to the top edge. Make four corner units measuring 9¼" square, including seam allowances.

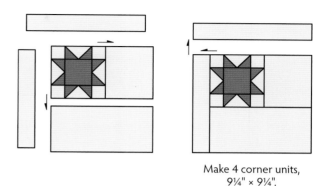

Make 4 corner units,
9¼" × 9¼".

**4.** Lay out the four star-point units to form a star, adding the corner units as shown. On the wrong side of each corner unit, mark the innermost corner ¼" from the raw edge in preparation for Y-seam construction. Join the star-point units in pairs, starting at the ¼" marks with a backstitch and sewing to the outside edge to make two half-star units. Join the half-star units, starting with a backstitch at the ¼" mark and stopping at the opposite mark with a backstitch. Press all seam allowances open.

red 1¾" × 13¼" strips as shown. Sew the strips together to make a strip set measuring 4¼" × 42", including seam allowances. Make a total of nine strip sets. Cut the strip sets into 172 segments, 1¾" × 4¼".

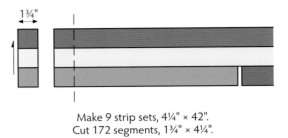

Make 9 strip sets, 4¼" × 42".
Cut 172 segments, 1¾" × 4¼".

**2.** Sew a cream small triangle to each end of a segment from step 1 to make 172 units. Press, making sure all the seam allowances are going in the same direction.

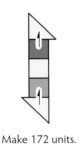

Make 172 units.

**3.** For the inner checkerboard border, join 15 units from step 2 to make a strip, rotating the units as needed to create opposing seam allowances. Make four strips.

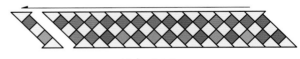

Make 4 strips.

**4.** Lay out four assorted red 1¾" squares, two cream 1¾" squares, and four cream small triangles in diagonal rows as shown. Sew the pieces into rows and then join the rows to make an end unit. Make eight.

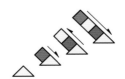 

Make 8 end units.

**5.** Place a corner unit on top of a diamond unit, right sides together and matching the ¼" marks. Starting with a backstitch at the ¼" mark, sew to the outside edge. In the same way, sew the corner unit to the adjacent diamond unit. Repeat to add the remaining corner units. The center Star block should measure 30½" square, including seam allowances.

Make 1 Center Star block,
30½" × 30½".

## Making the Checkerboard Borders

**1.** Arrange one of the assorted red 1¾" × 42" strips, one cream 1¾" × 42" strip, and three different assorted

**5.** Join an end unit to the left end of a strip from step 3 to make the top border. Repeat to make the bottom border. In the same way, make two side borders. Trim the triangles on each end of the side borders as shown, making sure to leave a ¼" seam allowance beyond the points of the red squares.

Make 2 top/bottom borders.

Make 2 side borders.

**6.** For the outer checkerboard border, join 28 units from step 2 to make a strip, rotating the units as needed to create opposing seam allowances. Make four strips. Repeat step 5 to sew an end unit to each strip and then trim the triangles on two of the borders.

Make 2 top/bottom borders.

Make 2 side borders.

**7.** Lay out six assorted red 1¾" squares, three cream 1¾" squares, and seven cream small triangles in diagonal rows as shown. Sew the pieces into rows and then join the rows to make a corner unit. Trim the triangle in the right-angle corner, making sure to leave a ¼" seam allowance beyond the point of the red square. Make eight units.

 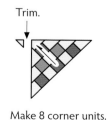

Make 8 corner units.

## Adding Borders 1–3

**1.** Sew the cream 1½" × 30½" strips to the left and right sides of the center Star block. Sew the cream 1½" × 32½" strips to the top and bottom edges. The quilt top should measure 32½" square, including seam allowances.

**2.** Sew the side inner checkerboard borders to the left and right sides of the quilt top. Sew the top and bottom inner checkerboard borders to the quilt top and bottom edges. Sew a checkerboard corner unit to each corner. The quilt top should measure 39½" square, including seam allowances.

**3.** Sew the cream 1½" × 39½" strips to the left and right sides of the quilt top. Join three cream 1½"-wide strips end to end. From the pieced strip, cut two 41½"-long strips and sew them to the top and bottom edges. The quilt top should measure 41½" square, including seam allowances.

Adding the borders

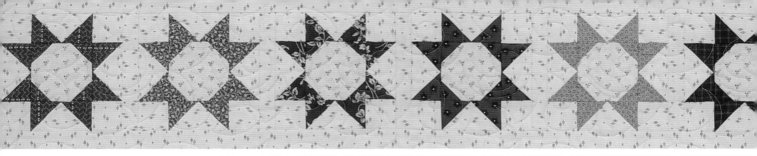

# Making the Star Border

**1.** Draw a diagonal line from corner to corner on the wrong side of four matching 1½" squares from the assorted red prints. Place a marked square on each corner of an ecru 3½" square. Sew on the marked lines. Trim the excess corner fabric ¼" from the stitched lines. Repeat to make a total of 28 center units measuring 3½" square, including seam allowances.

Make 28 center units,
3½" × 3½".

**2.** Draw a diagonal line from corner to corner on the wrong side of eight matching 2" squares from the assorted red prints. Place a marked square on one end of a cream 2" × 3½" piece, right sides together. Sew on the marked line. Trim the excess corner fabric ¼" from the stitched line. Place a marked square on the opposite end of the cream piece. Sew and trim as before to make a flying-geese unit measuring 2" × 3½", including seam allowances. Make 28 sets of four matching units.

Make 28 units,
2" × 3½".

**3.** Lay out four cream 2" squares, four matching flying-geese units, and a matching center unit in three rows. Sew the squares and units into rows. Join the rows to make a block. Make 28 blocks measuring 6½" square, including seam allowances.

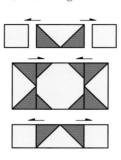 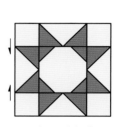

Make 28 blocks,
6½" × 6½".

**4.** Join six blocks and five cream 1¼" × 6½" strips to make a side border. Make two borders, adding a cream 1⅛" × 6½" strip to each end. The side borders should measure 6½" × 41½", including seam allowances. Join eight blocks, five cream 1¼" × 6½" strips, and two cream 1⅛" × 6½" strips to make the top border. Repeat to make the bottom border. The top and bottom borders should measure 6½" × 53½", including seam allowances.

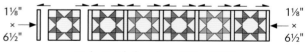

Make 2 side borders, 6½" × 41½".

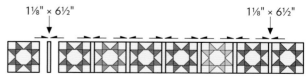

Make 2 side borders, 6½" × 53½".

**5.** Referring to the quilt assembly diagram on page 95, sew the borders to the left and right sides and then to the top and bottom edges of the quilt. The quilt top should measure 53½" square, including seam allowances.

## Adding the Remaining Borders

**1.** Join the remaining cream 1½"-wide strips end to end. From the pieced strip, cut two 55½"-long strips and two 53½"-long strips. Sew the shorter strips to the left and right sides of the quilt. Sew the longer strips to the top and bottom edges. The quilt top should measure 55½" square, including seam allowances.

**2.** Referring to the quilt assembly diagram, sew the side outer checkerboard borders to the quilt top and then add the top and bottom outer checkerboard borders. Sew a checkerboard corner unit to each corner. Press the seam allowances toward the corner units. The quilt top should measure 62½" square, including seam allowances.

**3.** Join the cream 3"-wide strips end to end. From the pieced strip, cut two 67½"-long strips and two 62½"-long strips. Sew the shorter strips to the left and right sides of the quilt top. Sew the longer strips to the top and bottom edges. The quilt top should measure 67½" square.

## Finishing the Quilt

For more details on any finishing steps, visit ShopMartingale.com/HowtoQuilt for free downloadable information.

**1.** Layer the quilt top with batting and backing; baste the layers together.

**2.** Quilt by hand or machine. Karen Styles machine quilted the quilt shown with an allover swirl design.

**3.** Use the red check 2½"-wide strips to make double-fold binding. Attach the binding to the quilt.

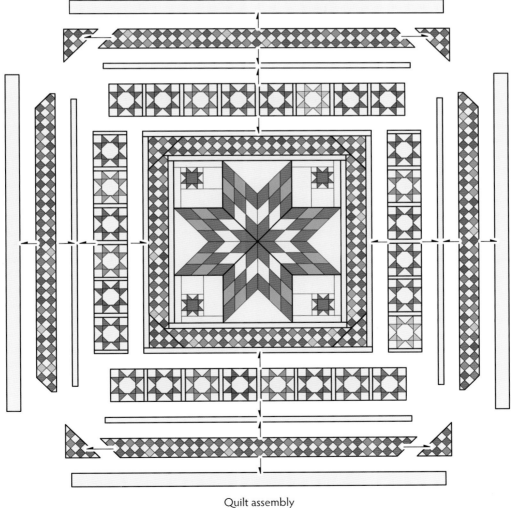

Quilt assembly

# ABOUT THE CONTRIBUTORS

◆ ◆ ◆ ◆ ◆

## SUSAN ACHE

Having always loved handwork and embroidery, Susan designs and creates quilts using everyday life as her inspiration and fabric as her playground.

## LISSA ALEXANDER

By day, Lissa heads up the Moda marketing team. By night, she's quilting, blogging, designing, and more at ModaLissa.com. Her wish? "I hope you get time to sit and sew. It's good for the soul."

## LISA BONGEAN

Lisa owns Primitive Gatherings Quilt Shop and is a designer for Moda Fabrics. She teaches and shares her designs across the country. You can find her at LisaBongean.com.

## JESSICA DAYON

Jessica Dayon is a fabric lover, wife, and mother of four. She enjoys quilting, pattern designing, and blogging. Check out her quilt-alongs and more at JessicaDayon.blogspot.com.

## JENNIFER KELTNER

Jennifer has been a maker of things from a very early age. As Martingale's publisher, she is as passionate as ever about all things fabric, quilting, embroidering, and sewing— always trying to squeeze a little "making" into every day.

## NANCY MARTIN

Nancy Martin and her husband Dan are the founders of Martingale, publisher of this book and hundreds of other quality quilting and craft books. Although retired from Martingale, Nancy still loves to quilt. She's also an avid gardener and professes that red is her favorite color!

## SHERRI MCCONNELL

Sherri received her first sewing machine when she was about 10 years old and has been sewing clothing and home-decor items ever since. After a gentle push from her grandmother, she branched out into quilting and hasn't stopped. Visit AQuiltingLife.com.

## DEBBIE ROBERTS

Debbie owns the Quilted Moose, a thriving shop in Gretna, Nebraska. She loves buying, displaying, and selling fabrics. Visit her at QuiltedMoose.com.

## GERRI ROBINSON

Gerri Robinson is both a quilt and a fabric designer who produces fabric lines for Riley Blake. She hails from Ohio, and you can find more about Gerri and her designs at PlantedSeedDesigns.com

## JODY SANDERS

Jody Sanders is the editor of American Patchwork & Quilting magazine. In addition to being a decades-long quilter, she is an avid collector of antique quilts and vintage sewing tools.

## PAT SLOAN

Pat Sloan is known to quilters worldwide as a quilt designer, author, teacher, YouTuber, and fabric designer. She hosts a very active and friendly quilting community on Facebook called Quilt Along with Pat Sloan, where she hosts many fun events. Find her at PatSloan.com.

## HELEN STUBBINGS

Helen is a fabric and pattern designer under the brand Hugs 'n Kisses. She owns and runs Quarter Inch Quilt Shop & Café in Hobart, Tasmania, when she's not traveling to teach around the world. Her passion is the therapy of stitching. Visit HugsnKisses.net

## KAREN STYLES

Karen says, "The color red is my favorite color. And a little-known fact about me is that I only ever wear red shoes." Visit her at SomersetPatchwork.com.au.